The KidHaven Science Library

Life Cycles

by Wendy Lanier

KIDHAVEN PRESS

An imprint of Thomson Gale, a part of The Thomson Corporation

THOMSON

GALE

Detroit • New York • San Francisco • San Diego • New Haven, Conn. • Waterville, Maine • London • Munich

LIBRARY OF CONGRESS CATALOGING-IN-PUBLICATION DATA

Lanier, Wendy, 1963–
    Life Cycles / by Wendy Lanier.
        p. cm. — (The KidHaven science library)
    Includes bibliographical references and index.
    ISBN 0-7377-2073-5 (hardcover : alk. paper) 1. Life cycles (Biology)—Juvenile literature. I. Title. II. Series.
    QH501.L36 2006
    571.8—dc22
                                                          2005018968

Printed in the United States of America

Contents

Chapter 1

Plant Life Cycles

All living things go through different stages as they live out their lives. Together, these stages of life are called a **life cycle.** Beginning with birth and ending at death, the events in a life cycle are repeated in the same order, generation after generation.

Seeds

Most plant life cycles begin with seeds. Seeds contain root, stem, and leaf parts just waiting for the right conditions to make them germinate, or grow. They need water, sunshine, and the correct temperature. When a seed has all these things, it begins to grow, sending roots down into the soil to take in water and nutrients. The roots also provide support for the growing plant.

When the stem and leaf parts from a seed first appear above the surface of the soil, the plant is called a seedling. As the seedling grows it uses water, sunshine, carbon dioxide in the air, and special substances in its leaves to make its own food.

Only green plants have the ability to make their own food.

As plants grow they make flowers. Even though flowers are pretty to look at, their only real purpose is to make seeds. Each flower blossom is like a seed factory. Plants make seeds as part of their life cycle to create the next generation of plants.

Seeds are created through a process called pollination. The flowers of most plants are made up of both male and female parts. The female parts in the center of the flower are called pistils. The male parts that surround the center are called stamens. At the top of each stamen is a powdery substance called pollen that contains male sperm cells.

Pollination takes place when pollen is transferred from neighboring flowers by the wind or a visiting insect to the sticky top of the pistil, the stigma. The

A Seed Becomes a Plant

sperm cells that make up the pollen travel down the pistil to the ovary. The ovary is at the base of the pistil and contains eggs. There the sperm cells join with the eggs. This is called fertilization.

Fruits and Pods

Fertilized eggs become seeds. The seeds grow inside the flower's ovary even as the flower begins to die. The petals fall away and the ovary swells to form a protective barrier around the seeds. The protective barrier becomes a fruit or pod. Many of the plant parts we eat are fruits, pods, or seeds. For example,

Flowers Are Seed Factories

In a plant's life cycle, pollination and fertilization begin the process of creating seeds that will grow to become new plants.

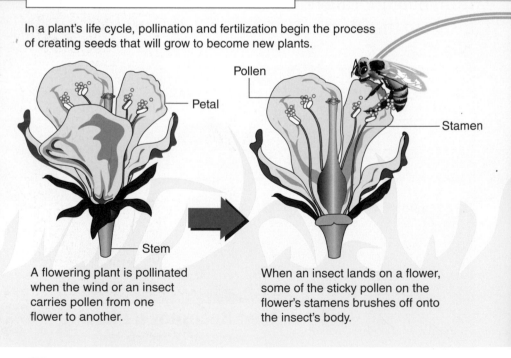

Pollen

Petal

Stamen

Stem

A flowering plant is pollinated when the wind or an insect carries pollen from one flower to another.

When an insect lands on a flower, some of the sticky pollen on the flower's stamens brushes off onto the insect's body.

corn kernels are seeds, bell peppers are pods, and apples are fruit.

When a fruit or pod ripens, the seeds are ready to become new plants. Sometimes the pods or fruit burst open and the seeds are scattered by the wind. At other times animals eat the fruit and the seeds are scattered in their droppings. Both people and animals can scatter seeds when seed pods stick to their clothing or fur and drop off later.

For some plants, once the seeds have been scattered, the plant's life cycle is nearing an end. Winter's freezing temperatures cause the plant to

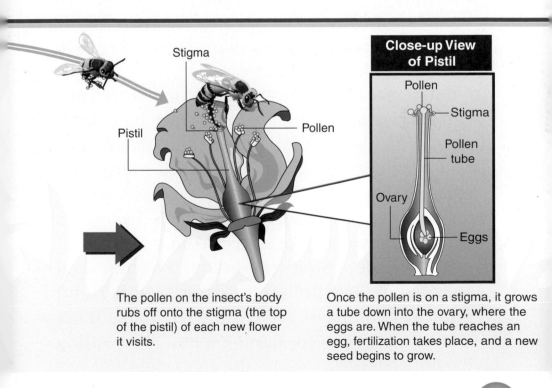

The pollen on the insect's body rubs off onto the stigma (the top of the pistil) of each new flower it visits.

Once the pollen is on a stigma, it grows a tube down into the ovary, where the eggs are. When the tube reaches an egg, fertilization takes place, and a new seed begins to grow.

die. At the beginning of the next growing season a whole new plant will grow from its seeds. These types of plants are called **annuals.** Vegetables such as sweet peas and corn are annuals. Flowers such as zinnias and sunflowers are annuals, too.

Other types of plants have much longer life cycles and produce flowers and seeds year after year. These plants are called **perennials.** Trees and bushes are good examples of perennials. While an annual's life cycle is completed in one growing season, a perennial's life cycle may continue for many years.

Conifers

One kind of perennial does not make flowers to reproduce. Instead these plants make cones. Plants that make cones, such as pine trees and spruce trees, are called **conifers.**

Conifers can grow in very harsh conditions. They can survive blistering heat and freezing cold in areas with little rainfall or constant high winds. Many conifers are commonly called evergreens because they do not lose their leaves during winter or dry seasons. They shed gradually over time, with new leaves appearing as old ones fall off.

Most conifers produce both pollen cones and seed cones. The pollen cones are smaller and grow at the tops of the trees. They make large amounts of pollen containing sperm. Each spring the pollen is released into the air as clouds of yel-

Conifers produce both seed cones and pollen cones like these.

low dust. Once the pollen is released, the pollen cones die.

The pollen dust is carried by the wind to the seed cones. When the pollen lands on the sticky surface of the seed cone, it sprouts and grows tubes to the eggs contained in the ovary. The ovary is buried deep in the center of the cone. There the eggs are fertilized and become seeds. The seeds develop on the scales, or petals, of the cone that grow around them as protection.

The new seeds are protected by the hard, woody scales of the cone. They remain there for several months or even years. While the seeds are forming the scales of the cone remain tightly closed. Finally,

Mosses grow stalks with pods that contain spores. Spores carried away on the wind grow into new mosses.

the cones open to reveal seeds with paperlike wings attached. The wings allow the seeds to be carried by the wind to a place where they can grow into new conifer plants.

Because conifers are perennials, they make seeds hundreds of times in their life span. Their life cycle is one of the longest among plants. Many conifers live to be thousands of years old.

Mosses

Some types of plants do not make flowers or seeds as a part of their life cycle. Mosses are one such group. More than 10,000 different kinds of mosses grow all over the world. Most of them grow in damp, shady places. They often look like leafy green mats or carpets growing on the ground, on rocks, or on fallen logs.

Mosses have special structures in their carpet of spongy green leaves that produce sperm and eggs. In the drops of moisture from rain or heavy dew, sperm swim to the eggs to fertilize them. The fertilized eggs produce stalks that grow up from the moss bed. At the tip of each stalk is a podlike cap that contains spores. When the conditions in the air are right, the spores are released to be carried by the wind. A spore is a single cell. If it lands in favorable conditions, the cell will divide and a new bed of moss will begin to grow.

Mosses usually live a long time. They can be dried out completely for long periods of time, sometimes years, and then restored to healthy growing plants with just a few drops of water. Some are known to be hundreds of years old.

Although there are many more kinds of animals than plants, plants are the basis for all life on this planet. They provide food, produce oxygen, and filter harmful substances out of the air. Without plants, animals could not survive.

Chapter 2

Animals That Undergo Change

Animal life cycles are more complicated than those of plants. Often, an animal's appearance changes dramatically as it grows from egg to adult. In each stage of development it looks very different. This change in appearance is called **metamorphosis.**

Salmon

Salmon are a kind of fish that go through metamorphosis. There are several types of salmon, but most of them live and hunt in the cold waters of the Northern Hemisphere.

Like most fish, salmon lay eggs to reproduce. A female salmon prepares a nest for her eggs along the bottom of the river where she was born. Usually a female deposits between 2,500 and 7,000 eggs into the nest, but some types of salmon can lay as many as 20,000 eggs.

As the female lays the eggs, the male swims directly behind her, depositing sperm to fertilize them. When fertilization is complete, the female covers the eggs with river rocks and sand by stirring up the stream bottom with her tail. Depending on the type of salmon, the eggs will hatch in two to six weeks.

Early Life

Newly hatched salmon are called alevins. The alevins remain in the nest for a time living off the food in a yolk sac attached to their belly. In about a month, all of the food in the sac has

(Below) When a female salmon lays her eggs, a male follows closely behind and fertilizes them. This is called spawning.

(Right) Newly hatched salmon get food from yolk sacs that are attached to their bellies.

been absorbed. The young fish, now called fry, are ready to strike out on their own.

When the fry leave their nest they are completely alone. Their parents do not take care of them. They survive entirely by **instinct**. Instincts are natural abilities or behaviors that help animals survive. They are not taught the behaviors but are born with them.

Growing to Adulthood

Salmon fry swim in rivers and streams for one to three years, feeding on tiny plants and small insects. They must hide under rocks and water plants to avoid being eaten themselves. Even at this

Adolescent salmon swim together in large groups called schools.

early stage they begin to **migrate**, or move, downstream toward the ocean.

By the time the fry are ready to venture out into the ocean they have reached **adolescence.** At this time they appear full grown but are still too young to reproduce. At this stage salmon are called smolt. Schooling together in large groups, the smolt swim out into the ocean to feed and grow into adult salmon.

After one to four years at sea the salmon reach adulthood and are finally ready to **spawn,** or reproduce. At that time they are driven by instinct back to the very stream in which they were born. Many scientists believe they find their way there by smell. Some salmon travel more than 1,000 miles (1,609 km) to reach their birthplace.

Many salmon die after they have spawned. Other species rest and then go back to sea. Some of them even return to spawn again. These oceangoing salmon can live to be seven or eight years old.

Salmon are not the only living things whose appearance changes as they grow to adulthood. Insects are another example of animals that go through metamorphosis.

A Long Life Cycle

Most insects have very short life cycles. Many live only a few weeks at the most. Cicadas, however, are unusual because theirs is the longest life cycle in the insect world.

This life cycle begins with eggs deposited by female cicadas in slits they make in the branches of living plants. About six weeks after they are deposited, the eggs begin to hatch. Tiny wormlike **larvae** with big black eyes drop to the ground and begin to burrow into the soil. There they feed on tree roots.

At this stage, the cicadas are called nymphs. Underground, they shed their skin several times as they grow, looking more and more like adult cicadas with each shedding. Finally, after feeding underground for seventeen years, the nymphs crawl out of the ground and up the nearest vertical surface.

The Cycle Ends

At this point, the cicadas shed for the last time. A split appears along the back of each insect and a winged adult cicada emerges. Leaving behind a life-like shell, each cicada flies off to find a mate.

During mating, a male cicada vibrates tendons under two small plates on its underside to produce a mating call that will attract a female. Thousands of cicadas all making this noise at once can create quite a racket. Their shrill song often fills the air in the early morning and late evening.

Once they have mated, the male cicadas die. The females live only long enough to lay their eggs. Six weeks later, with the hatching of the eggs, the seventeen-year life cycle begins again.

Cicadas develop underground for seventeen years before coming to the surface. When they emerge, they shed their skin before flying off in search of mates.

Like cicadas, honeybees are insects that go through metamorphosis. For honeybees, however, the cycle is much shorter.

Honeybees live and work in groups called colonies. Three kinds of bees live in a colony: workers, drones, and a single queen. Workers are female bees who take care of the hive and help the queen, who lays eggs. The queen is the only female that does this. Drones are male bees.

All three kinds of bees begin their life cycle as eggs. An adult queen lays the eggs in the bottom of small,

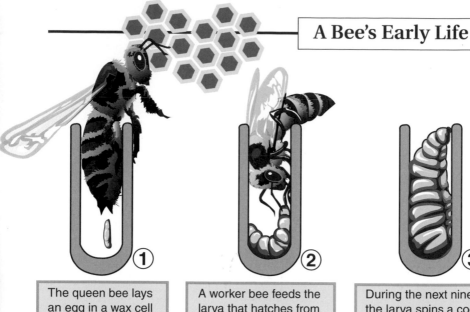

1. The queen bee lays an egg in a wax cell inside the hive.

2. A worker bee feeds the larva that hatches from the egg.

3. During the next nine days, the larva spins a cocoon and develops to full size.

hexagon-shaped chambers in the honeycomb. After three days, larvae hatch from the eggs. The larvae are cared for and fed by worker bees. Queen larvae are fed a substance called royal jelly, or bee's milk. Worker bee and drone larvae are fed mostly beebread (made of collected pollen and honey).

After about nine days the larvae spin cocoons. Inside the cocoons, the larvae develop into **pupae.** They develop eyes, legs, and wings. By this time, they look nothing like the tiny worms that hatched from the eggs. The pupae that become queens take about six days to fully develop. Worker bees take eleven days and drones take fourteen.

When a pupa is finished growing, it chews its way out of the honeycomb chamber. What the newborn

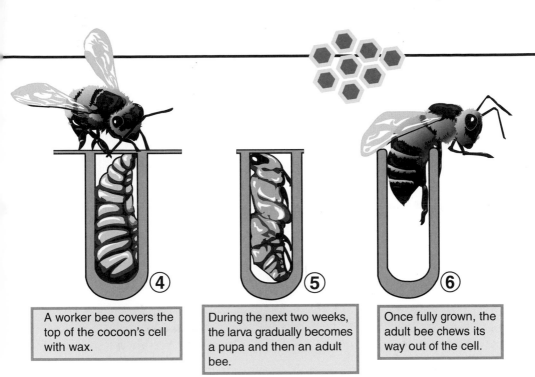

④ A worker bee covers the top of the cocoon's cell with wax.

⑤ During the next two weeks, the larva gradually becomes a pupa and then an adult bee.

⑥ Once fully grown, the adult bee chews its way out of the cell.

bee does next depends on whether it is a worker, drone, or queen bee.

Most of the bees in a colony are worker bees. The minute a worker bee is born, she begins to work. She spends the first three weeks of her life cleaning the hive, feeding the larvae, building wax honeycombs, storing food, and defending the hive. None of the other bees teach her to do this. She does it all by instinct.

After three weeks, a worker bee becomes a field bee. She begins her new job by making about ten trips a day to gather nectar, pollen, bee glue (sap), and water. In summer she visits nearly 6,000 flowers a day to collect these things. She works so hard that she lives only about six weeks. During the winter, when there are fewer flowers to visit, worker bees may live several months. No matter in which season worker bees live, they do not stop their work until they die.

While the worker bees do all the work, the drones do very little. Their only job is to mate with the queen. They are usually born at the beginning of summer for this purpose. By September, because they do nothing else to contribute to the success of the colony, they are pushed out of the hive to die.

The Queen's Life Cycle

The life cycle of a queen is different from those of workers and drones. Normally, as soon as a queen hatches, her first job is to get rid of her competition. She does this by stinging and killing the existing queen, as well as any other queen larvae that have not yet hatched.

Once her place as queen has been established, the new queen flies off to join the drones in a mating flight. During the flight she mates with a dozen or more drones. When the flight is completed she returns to the hive to begin laying eggs. She does not mate again but spends the rest of her life laying eggs and being cared for by workers. A healthy queen may live as long as four years and lay over 1 million eggs.

Change is a normal part of the life cycle in all animals. In animals that go through metamorphosis, the changes are especially dramatic.

Chapter 3

Animals That Lay Eggs

Most animals, including birds, insects, reptiles, amphibians, and fish, lay eggs. Many lay their eggs and then leave their offspring to survive on their own. Those that do this usually produce many eggs. This is nature's way of making sure that at least some of the young will survive to adulthood.

Other animals care for both their eggs and the hatched offspring until they can care for themselves. Those that tend their young usually have only a few babies at a time. This way the parents can provide proper care while teaching the babies the things they need to know to survive.

Penguins

Penguins are one example of an animal that lays eggs and then takes care of its young. These birds spend about 80 percent of their time at sea. They do not fly but are talented swimmers.

There are seventeen different species of penguins. Two of them live on the continent of Antarctica. One of the two, the emperor penguin, is the largest of the penguin family. It can reach 45 inches (114cm) in height and weighs about 65 pounds (29kg).

Each year, in April, winter is just getting under-way near the Antarctic. While other animals are

To reach their nesting site, emperor penguins may walk more than 50 miles in the coldest place on earth.

migrating to warmer places, the emperor penguins are just arriving. Their nesting time is in the middle of winter in the coldest place on Earth. Because of all the ice they must sometimes walk more than 50 miles (80km) to reach the nesting site. There they gather in colonies that can number over 100,000 birds.

Tending the Chick

Sometime in May, after mating, the female emperor penguin lays a single egg, which the male immediately takes over. He places the egg on top of his webbed feet and wraps a fold of his belly around it like a feather blanket. This is his brood pouch. For the next two months, about 63 days, the male stands in the freezing Antarctic winds keeping the egg warm, or **incubating** it. He does not eat for the entire time.

Meanwhile, the female makes the long trip back to the sea, walking over what is now up to 70 miles (100km) of ice to reach the ocean. In July, she returns to the nesting colony with her crop, a pouch in her throat, filled with food for the chick that is ready to hatch. By this time the male has lost more than half of his body weight. The female immediately takes over the care of the chick so that the male can return to the ocean to feed. Like his mate, the male returns with a crop full of food for the new chick.

The penguin chicks rely on their parents to care for them for the next five to six months. This period of time is called **brooding.** During that time the parents take turns caring for the chick.

By late spring, November and December, the chicks in the colony are old enough for their parents to leave them alone together in groups while they are away on hunting trips. In January, when summer begins, the chicks have shed their baby feathers and grown new, waterproof feathers that will allow them to stay warm and dry in water. They strike out for the ocean with their parents, where they learn to hunt and swim.

After about four years of swimming and hunting in the cold ocean depths, the chicks are full grown and ready to mate. For the next fifteen to twenty years, their summers are spent at sea. Each winter they return to land to raise a single chick, often with the same mate.

Sea Turtles

In contrast to penguins, most reptiles never even see their young. Like birds, most reptiles lay eggs, but they are rarely around to see them hatch. Their young are left to survive completely on their own. Sea turtles are one example.

Under cover of night, a female sea turtle crawls slowly out of the waves onto a beach. She returns to the same beach, sometimes the very spot, where

A female emperor penguin lays only a single egg in a season. After it hatches, the male and female take turns caring for the chick.

she was born herself. It may be the first time she has been back in more than twenty years.

Finding a suitable spot above the high tide line, the female digs a hole. In it, she deposits 100 or more eggs about the size and shape of ping-pong balls. The eggs are leathery, so they bounce rather than break as they fall into the hole.

When she is finished, the female covers the group of eggs, or **clutch**, with sand and then lumbers back

A sea turtle crawls onto the beach to lay its eggs in the sand.

to the sea. While they do not nest every year, sea turtles may nest up to seven times in a single nesting season. By the end of the season one female may lay as many as 1,000 eggs in several clutches.

For the next 55 days or so, depending on the temperature, the eggs incubate in the sand. Scientists believe that the temperature of the nest affects whether the hatchlings will be male or female. Cooler temperatures result in more males. Warmer temperatures mean more females.

The Turtles Hatch

When the incubation is complete, the eggs hatch under the warm sand. On a clear night, the hatchlings dig out of the hole together and instinctively race toward the ocean where the moonlight sparkles on the water. At only about 2 inches (5cm) long, the tiny turtles are often preyed upon by birds and small animals. Those turtles that manage to make it to the water must swim hard to reach the safety of floating seaweed. There they can hide and feed on small marine animals that live in the seaweed.

Not much is known about what the hatchlings do for the first few years. Scientists call them the "lost years" because they have no idea how the tiny turtles survive in the ocean. It is a long time before the hatchlings are large enough to swim in open water. Scientists estimate that only 1 or 2 hatchlings out

(Above) Female sea turtles lay 100 or more eggs at a time.

(Right) A sea turtle hatches.

of 100 survive one year. Only 1 in 1,000 (maybe even 10,000) survive long enough to reproduce.

In ten to fifteen years, the hatchlings that survive finally reach adulthood. As adults, they are ready to mate and can be quite large. An adult loggerhead turtle, for example, weighs 200 to 300 pounds (91 to 159kg) and is about 3 feet (1m) long. Once they have made it to this size, they have few enemies. Although very few sea turtles live to be adults, those that do can live to be as much as 100 years old.

A Life at Sea

Male sea turtles do not return to land again in their lifetime. The females return only to lay their eggs every two to three years. Other than that, their entire life cycle is spent at sea.

Sea turtles are just one example of animals that lay many eggs. The more eggs an animal lays, the less likely it is to care for its young. Animals that lay only one or very few eggs are likely to feed, protect, and care for their young until they are able to take care of themselves.

Chapter 4

Animals That Bear Live Young

While birds, insects, reptiles, amphibians, and fish all lay eggs, another group of animals does not. These animals are known as mammals. Instead of laying eggs, female mammals give birth to live young.

Elephants and Humans

Mammals come in all shapes and sizes. For example, elephants and humans are both mammals. The two do not appear to be very similar at first glance. Elephants are the largest mammals that live on land. A full-grown African elephant can be anywhere from 7 to 13 feet (2 to 4m) tall and weigh nearly 12,000 pounds (5,440kg). The average adult human male, by contrast, is only 5 feet 8 inches to 5 feet 10 inches (173 to 177cm) tall and weighs about 175 pounds (79kg).

Even though elephants and humans look nothing alike, they have things in common with each

Like other mammals, a baby elephant is completely dependent on its mother for food.

other and with all other mammals. Mammal eggs are fertilized inside the body of the female during mating. In the very early stages of their development, all mammals look alike. The female continues to carry the developing young inside her body until they are born. The time it takes for the young to grow large enough to be born is called gestation.

Baby elephants, called calves, are born after a gestation of two years. This is the longest gestation period of any animal. Like other mammals, newborn calves look just like their parents, only smaller.

Elephants live in groups called herds that are similar to human families. Adult elephants protect and teach the young calves.

Calves are born under the watchful eyes of the other females, called cows, in the mother's **herd.** A herd is a family group much like a human family. All of the cows in the herd help the mother care for her new baby. As with humans, elephant mothers usually give birth to only one calf at a time.

Early Years

At first, calves depend entirely on their mothers' milk for food. After about three months, they begin learning to graze, even though they may continue to nurse for up to four years.

A calf's first few years are spent learning all about being an elephant. Other herd members show it how to find tender grass to eat, seek shelter in the heat of the day, and cool off in a mud wallow. Both male and female calves stay with their mother's herd until they reach adolescence, sometime between ages eight and thirteen.

About the time they reach adolescence, male elephants, called bulls, leave the herd to join male-only herds. From then on, the young bulls spend most of their time in the all-male herds unless they are in search of a mate. Female elephants continue to live in the herd with their mother and other females from their family for their entire lives.

Much like humans, both bulls and cows reach sexual maturity, a stage when they are physically ready to reproduce, during their adolescence. For

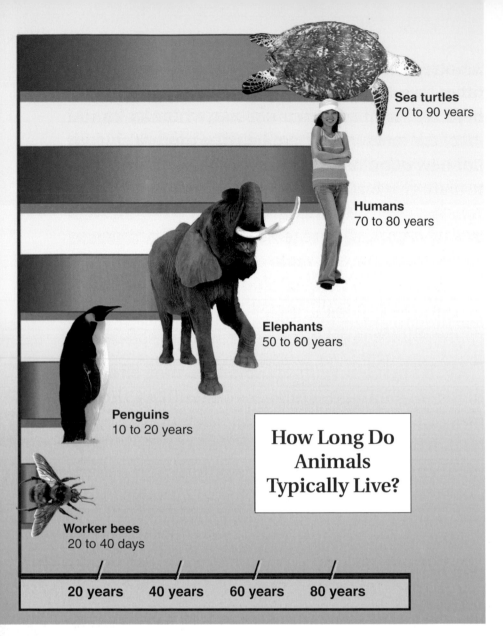

How Long Do Animals Typically Live?

Sea turtles
70 to 90 years

Humans
70 to 80 years

Elephants
50 to 60 years

Penguins
10 to 20 years

Worker bees
20 to 40 days

| 20 years | 40 years | 60 years | 80 years |

the bulls this is usually at about thirteen. Cows are usually ready to bear young by about age sixteen. Once a cow begins reproducing she generally gives birth every two and one-half to four years.

Elephant adult years begin at the age of 20. Between the ages of 20 and 40, they are at their strongest and healthiest. After age 40, as they get older, they begin to slow down. Like humans, an elephant may experience age-related diseases such as arthritis or heart disease as they age.

The length of an elephant's life cycle is ultimately determined by its teeth. Elephants have six sets of teeth for a total of 24. Only four teeth are in use at any one time. As the teeth in use are worn down, they fall out and are replaced by the next teeth in line. When the last set of teeth is lost the elephant is not able to chew properly. It can no longer feed

A human develops inside its mother's body. This photo shows a six-week-old human embryo.

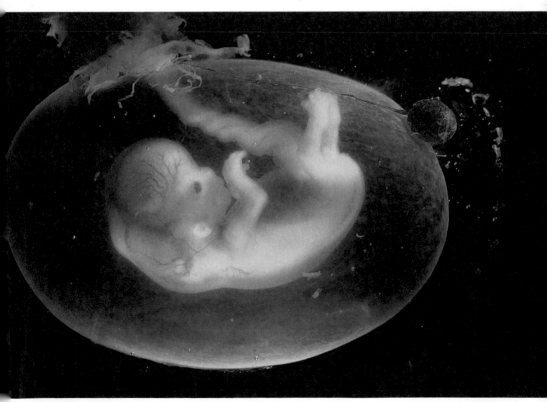

Infancy

Childhood

Adolescence

Adulthood

itself and eventually dies of starvation. Unless it is killed by an illegal hunter or something unusual happens, an elephant has a life cycle of about 50–60 years, some living as long as 70 years. This is about the same as a human's.

Like that of elephants, the human life cycle begins when an egg in the body of a female is fertilized by sperm from a male. At the moment of fertilization all of the information about the infant's gender, hair color, eye color, physical features, and even most personality traits is set.

The gestation period for humans is usually 38 to 40 weeks. During this time, the baby grows from a tiny speck to an average of 20 inches (51cm) long and weighs about 7 pounds (3kg) at birth. It is born completely helpless and is dependent on its parents to feed and care for it.

A Baby Grows Up

The first few years of a human baby's life are filled with learning. The baby must learn to crawl, stand, walk, and talk. By the time babies reach the toddler stage, at three years old, they can tell their age in years, walk upright, and easily climb stairs. During the next few years, the child continues to grow and learn quickly. Some scientists believe that human beings learn half of everything they will learn in their lifetime by the time they have completed the toddler stage.

In most cultures, by the age of five or six a child is learning to read and write. Most have started school or some other form of education and are learning new things every day. Unlike the physical learning of the toddler years, these childhood years are filled with mental learning.

At the age of thirteen or so, a child reaches adolescence. During the adolescent, or teenage, years the child matures physically and reaches his or her full height. These years are often very emotional ones as the young person tries to adjust to the way his or her body is changing. Teenagers may experience acne and growth spurts. Boys usually develop deeper voices, while girls gain extra weight and develop breasts.

At eighteen to twenty years, adulthood is just beginning. The early adult years are often called the "prime of life." Under normal circumstances

With each new generation, the human cycle of life begins again.

this is the time when a human is strongest and most capable mentally. Women between the ages of 18 and 30 are more likely to have children than any other age group.

The Later Years

By age 40, humans are considered to be in their middle-age years. The signs of aging, such as wrinkles, gray hair, and loss of strength, are becoming more noticeable. Even so, most people still enjoy a good quality of life.

When humans reach the age of 60, they enter their old age. The quality of their life is determined by the lifestyle they have had until this point. A healthful lifestyle helps to assure them of a healthy life in their later years. Eating a balanced diet, exercising, and participating in mental activities all contribute to a healthy body after age 60.

Although the life cycle of humans today lasts an average of about 70 years, that number is higher in countries that have good health care and clean living conditions. In the United States the average life span is about 77 years. In Japan the average is over 80. In most countries, women have a slightly higher average life span than men.

Human beings, like all other life forms on Earth, have a cycle of life. The cycle begins with their birth and is complete at their death. Each new generation begins a new cycle.

Glossary

adolescence: The part of an animal's life cycle in which it is almost fully grown but not yet an adult.

annuals: Plants that live for only one year or growing season.

brooding: The care and feeding of an animal's offspring, especially birds that are hatched at the same time and cared for together.

clutch: A nest of eggs.

conifers: Any cone-bearing tree or shrub, mostly evergreens.

herd: A group of cattle or other large animals that live and graze together.

incubating: Keeping eggs warm and in a favorable environment for hatching.

instinct: A natural behavior for survival; one that does not have to be learned.

larvae: The early form or stage of insects before they change into adults, usually through a dramatic change in appearance.

life cycle: A series of physical changes and events in the life of a living thing from its earliest stages of development to its death.

metamorphosis: A complete change in form, shape, or function in a living thing as it progresses from its earliest stages of life to adulthood.

migrate: To move from one location to another to live, usually influenced by seasons or food supply.

perennials: Plants with a life cycle of more than two years that produce flowers and seeds from the same root structure each year.

pupae: Animals in a nonfeeding stage between the larva stage and adulthood, often taking place in cocoons.

spawn: Producing or depositing eggs or sperm, usually in great quantity.

Books

Kris Hirshmann, *Sea Turtles.* San Diego: KidHaven, 2005. This is an "everything you ever wanted to know" kind of book. It describes where sea turtles are found, what they look like, how they reproduce and nest, and how they find food. It also includes information about efforts to protect this endangered animal.

Lisa Magloff, *Elephant.* New York: DK, 2005. Fabulous photography shows the growth of a newborn elephant to an adult.

Charles Micucci, *The Life and Times of the Honeybee.* Boston: Houghton Mifflin, 1995. A lot goes on in a bee colony. This book has all the details about bees and their activities. It has lots of interesting facts with excellent illustrations.

Cynthia Moss, *Elephant Memories.* Chicago: University of Chicago Press, 2000. First printed in Canada in 1988, this book was reprinted in 2000 with a new afterword by the author. Wonderful photographs, many taken by the author, and a story-like text tell all about elephant life in the wild.

Web Sites

Enchanted Learning (www.enchantedlearning. com). This site now has a small annual fee, but it has lots of fun animal printouts. There are 25 different pages of animal life cycles.

Life Cycle Site List (www.oswego.org/staff/ccham ber/resources/lifecycle.cfm). This is a great resource that has a whole list of sites about animal life cycles with links to each.

Life Cycles of Living Things (www.lakeland schools.org/EDTECH/teacher/LTPM/lifecycles.ht ml). This is a great site designed by a teacher and includes other Web sites to visit, activities to do, and even a quiz to see what you know.

Utah Education Network: Cycles in Nature (www.uen.org/themepark/cycles). This site discusses the cycles of plants, animals, and even non-living things.

Index

Wendy Lanier is a teacher, author, and speaker who lives in Beaumont, Texas, with her husband, a daughter who is ten, and three dogs. She writes and speaks on a variety of topics for students and adults.